Learn H[...]
PAINT [...]

Traditional
SIGNWRITING
Freestyle Guide

© Wayne Tanswell 2010

First published in Great Britain by
Tanswell Publications 2010
4 Kersey Avenue, Great Cornard, Sudbury, Suffolk CO10 0DZ

Printed by
The Lavenham Press Ltd
Arbons House, 47 Water Street, Lavenham, Suffolk, CO10 9RN

ISBN No: 978-0-9562463-1-8

Acknowledgements

This book was produced with the full support of my home team:
Angi, Harriet, Travis and Dylan.

I am also grateful to the following:

Howard Sheldon (Editing)
Michael & Adam Venus (A S Handover)
Derek Pearson (Editor of Signworld Magazine)
My friend the English Dictionary

Also to those who commissioned the work featured in this book.

CONTENTS

About the Author

Suffolk is a county of great beauty. It is a rural environment that once inspired artists such as Thomas Gainsborough and is still a corner of England that might possibly convince an American tourist that they are liable to stumble across Miss Marple round every cobbled corner. So it is fitting that this is the home of traditional Signwriter Wayne Tanswell, a man that has hand lettered the lyrics of a Bob Dylan song around his living room walls and houses his workshop in the outbuildings of a farm.

His working day might find him in his workshop or out on site lettering signs for a top-notch London pub, but it always finds him doing the thing he loves most. This passion for sign writing started on the very day he left school at the age of 16 and accepted a lift from Sudbury to Long Melford with a signwriter who was looking for an apprentice. He made his first sign in 1980, the same year he created the logo for his new wave rock group, "Utter Chaos".

Now the band is just a memory, as is the mop of curly hair we see in the yellowed newspaper from 30 years ago. His love for music remains, the skills and techniques he started learning then as a signwriter have since been developed to a master pitch and what is more, Wayne is now ready to share them with others.

Suffolk Free Press, Thursday, December 11, 1980 11

This book is not a new development as, in 1994 he made a tuition video that demonstrated his craft and in 2009, Wayne launched his first book, *Learn How To Paint Signs*, a traditional signwriting introductory guide.

Derek Pearson Editor of SIGNWORLD Magazine

Freestyle Introduction

The purpose of the 'Freestyle Guide' is to follow on from the knowledge and skills gained from the 'Introductory Guide', and progress onto Script, Old English and Roman lettering. I recapitulate on important areas and concentrate on developing freestyle lettering, spacing and designing techniques. The Freestyle Guide is designed to challenge your knowledge and observation and to work out letter combinations from the basic and italic brush stroke charts.

I have designed a user friendly chart consisting of four colours to assist in building letters.

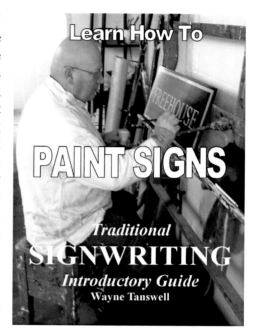

`Learn How To Paint Signs`
Traditional Signwriting Introductory Guide
Wayne Tanswell
ISBN No: 9680956246301
Tanswell Publications

Every Signwriter paints differently. Even if we all have the same information, we are not machines programmed for perfection.
When commissioned to paint a sign and the font requirements are either, Script, Old English or Roman, we paint our interpretation that is both unique and of a high standard.
The information in this book encourages you to develop your own freestyle way of signwriting within the boundaries of conventional typefaces.
Slight imperfections are tolerated, such as feathered edges and brush marks because they add character and authenticity to hand painted signs.

Recapitulate

1. Always use quality brushes made of Sable, Red Sable or Sable and Ox.
Quality brushes enable you to have neat edges to your letters. They also hold a good amount of paint to help with the one stroke techniques.

2. To keep your brushes soft, clean thoroughly, then wipe the hair in clear multi-purpose grease, finally nip the hair together in a chisel shape.
When you are ready to use the brush again, wipe the grease off onto a rag and then clean thoroughly in white spirit.
Your brush will be soft and ready for use.
The brushes used for the techniques

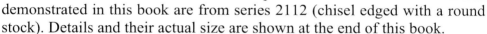
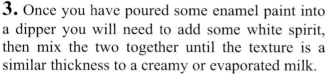

demonstrated in this book are from series 2112 (chisel edged with a round stock). Details and their actual size are shown at the end of this book.

3. Once you have poured some enamel paint into a dipper you will need to add some white spirit, then mix the two together until the texture is a similar thickness to a creamy or evaporated milk.
By thinning the paint you avoid the brush dragging and your letters will flow smoothly without creating any feathered or jagged edges.
Depending on the weather conditions you may also need to add a reducer to the paint, because when it is cold the paint may run and when it is hot the paint may drag.
A low temperature reducer will accelerate the paint drying time and a high temperature reducer will slow down the paint drying time.
Only use reducers in extreme temperatures.

Work Upright

The main advantage for painting in an upright position is to maintain control of the brush.

Once the brush has been loaded with paint and wiped into a chisel edge shape, you have slightly more time to apply the paint to the surface before the brush looses its shape.

When working upright, keep the brush in a horizontal position for maximum brush control.

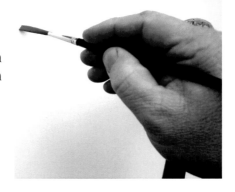

Of course there will be times when it isn't possible to work upright because some surfaces are flat. In these circumstances apply the paint at an increased speed.

Freestyle Brush Control

STEP 1.

Hold the brush at comfortable
writing angle

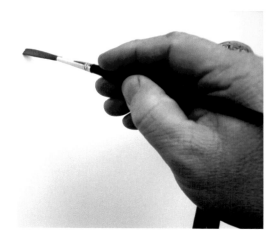

STEP 2.

Use the tip of the brush and drag
the brush up to the right

STEP 3.

Then twist round and drag
downwards, laying the brush flat.

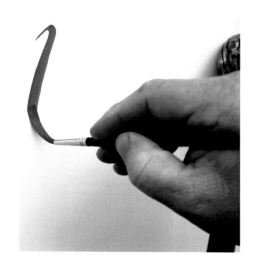

STEP 4.

Twist the brush to the right and drag upwards using the tip of the brush.

STEP 5.

Twist the brush back round and drag down, laying the brush flat the same as in step 3.

STEP 6.

Finally, drag the brush downwards.

If you have thinned the paint correctly, you should be able to paint all of these 6 steps in one continuous brushstroke.

Italic Brush Stroke Chart

You may need to adjust the height of these italic brush strokes to make different letters as demonstrated with brush stroke number one.

You can make any italic letter with these brush strokes.

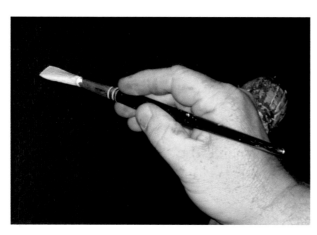

To create an Italic letter, hold the brush at a 45 degree angle.
You may find this type of lettering easier than the basic brush strokes.
Keep the tip of the brush chiselled at all times.
A lot of italics and scripts share the same brush strokes.

This style of the lettering means that the clean upstrokes are not needed so much as the basic brush strokes.

Colour Chart

Letters are made by painting various brushstrokes from the Italic and basic brushstroke charts.

This colour chart indicates the order in which to apply the brushstrokes for all of the exercises in this book.

For lettering and shading always paint from:

Top to bottom

Left to right

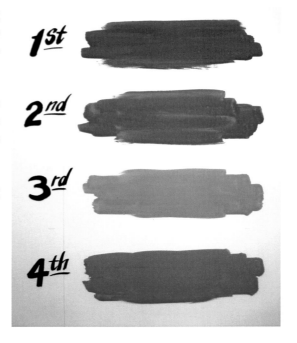

Chalk lines are used to set out fonts such as Script and Old English. These fonts have curved edges that need to flow without getting flat tops and bottoms to the letters which may be the result when using tape.

China Graph Pencils and Chalk are also used to draw most letters.

You can paint over the chalk or china graph markings. Any markings that are still visible once you have finished painting can be wiped off with white spirit when the letters have dried.

Script Lettering

The formation of script lettering comes from the italic brush strokes.

Letters are connected by painting a thin line from one letter to another allowing the words to flow. Script letters are created by painting thick and thin brush strokes from the italic chart.

The script font is used to add a look of quality and elegance to a sign. Script is also known as 'Palace Script' or 'English script'.

Hand painting script letters may look difficult, but it is probably one of the easiest fonts to paint and naturally develop your own style.

Use lower case when grouping letters into words because grouped capitals are illegible.

lower case **legible**

CAPITALS **illegible**

Script Alphabet

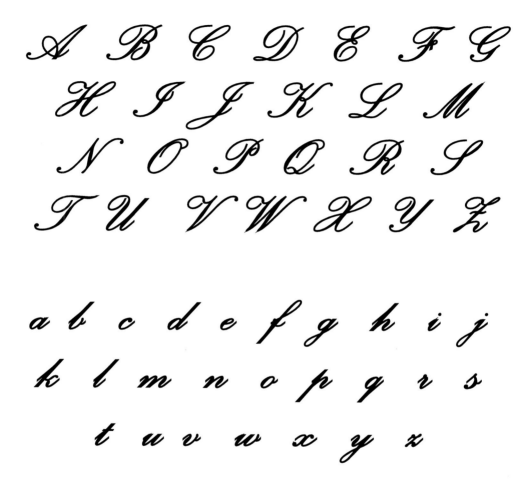

These letters are also from the italic brush stroke chart and should be joined by painting a thin line between each letter, grouping them into words. This technique is done by using the tip of the brush.

Use your skill and judgement to work out what combinations were used with the italic brush stroke chart to create these letters.

Script Colour Chart

Script

abc defg

hijklmno

pqrstuv

wxyz

Script and Old English Lettering

By observing the italic brush stroke chart you will see how Script and Old English letters formed. They are created by making slight alterations to the angle of brush strokes.

As there are many variations of Script and Old English, it is advisable to modify and develop your own freehand style.

Script

Script letters are joined by a thin brush stroke and look better as italics.

Old English

Use the edge of your brush for deviations such as thin lines and corner flicks. Old English letters look better upright.

Various combinations from the italic brush stroke chart are applied in order to form a single letter.

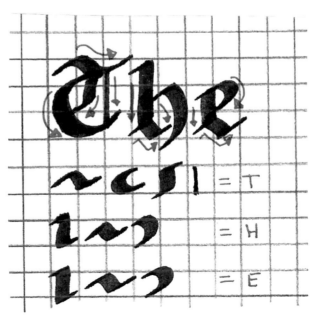

"Creativity is allowing yourself to make mistakes ...

the art in signwriting is knowing which ones to keep"

Old English Alphabet

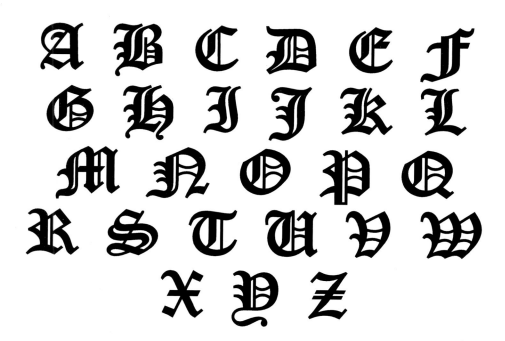

There are several variations of Old English.
History books show how it has changed several times during each century.
Use combinations from the italic chart to create Old English and modify it
to your own style.

Old English Lettering

The foundations of Old English letters comes from the Italic Brush strokes.

These chisel edged brush strokes are slightly adjusted to create Old English letters, which are also thick and thin brush strokes.

Use lower case when grouping letters as using only capitals can make a sign illegible.

This font creates a vintage and traditional look for a sign.

There are many variations of Old English to choose from and modify to your own style.

lower case legible

CAPITALS illegible

Old English Colour Chart

Roman Lettering

Roman letters are made of thick and thin brush strokes and have serifs.
'Serifs' are the small finishing strokes on the end of the letter.
'Sans Serif' letters do not have these finishing brush strokes.

Serifs   ## Sans Serif

Serif variations

1. **POINTED**

2. **ROUNDED**

3. **SQUARED**

The vertical strokes are painted thicker with two brush strokes and the horizontal strokes are a single brush stroke.

Basic Brush Stroke Chart

By using these six basic brush strokes you can make Roman letters in
both capitals and lower case.

Always start your brush stroke from the top of the letter including the curved brush strokes, also from left to right when painting the horizontal brush strokes.

This picture shows how to hold the brush for vertical, basic brush strokes, using a chisel edged round stock brush.

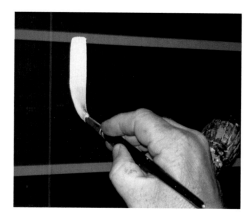

Make sure that the top of the brush is horizontal and brush down from the top of the letter.

Basic brush strokes: Capitals.
Use two lines of low tack tape at the top and bottom of the letter.

Basic brush strokes: Lower case.
Use four lines of low tack tape for this exercise

Roman Lettering

The foundation of Roman lettering comes from the six basic brush strokes.
By observing the basic brush stroke chart, you will see how the letters are created. Remember to paint horizontal lines thinner.

These letters demonstrate the vertical, curved and horizontal brush strokes.

As there are many variations of Roman lettering to choose from, it is advisable to modify and develop your own unique style.

Roman letters can be painted in groups of capitals as well as groups of lower case. Serif and Sans Serif fonts are legible in both upper and lower case and are widely used.

lower case legible

CAPITALS legible

Roman Colour Chart

Roman Alphabet

A B C D E F G H
I J K L M N O P
Q R S T U V W
X Y Z

a b c d e f g h i j k
l m n o p q r s t u v
w x y z

This is a standard chart for reference from which you can create your own versions. For example, this font can be painted bold, narrow or italic depending on what size brush you use.

Useful Tips

Spacing

Signs are more legible when there is space between lines of text on all sides.

It is important not to overcrowd your design.

You increase the visibility of a sign by decreasing the size of the letters

Shading

Emphasize important words that need to stand out. This can be achieved by changing the colours, underlining or adding a shade. By doing this you add depth and highlight the important words.

Shading also enhances words and makes then more readable from a distance.

Use this technique for impact and decoration.

Various Shading Techniques

A. Angle Drop Shade
B. Square Drop Shade
C. Touching Shade
D. Line & Shade

Useful Tips

Signs need to be clear and easy to read which means correctly laying out your design. Legible signs are created by closing awkward spaces.

Awkward Space   ## Corrected space

PARTY PARTY

Awkward spaces are mainly caused by these six capital letters:

A P T V L Y

Awkward spaces can also be found between capitals and lower case letters. Words become easier to read as a result of closing awkward gaps. The overlapping of words is an important technique and makes the signs more legible.

When we set out letters demonstrated in the `Introductory Guide`, we divided the amount of letters by the width of the sign into spaces. However, spacing letters is not always mathematically equal.

For example, the letter 'I' only uses approximately ½ the width of a normal letter space.

The letters 'W' and 'M' take up more width, usually 1½ times the width of a normal letter space.

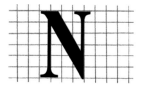

Block and Roman lettering usually looks best when the height is 1 ½ times the width. This creates the best proportion and appearance.

The Ampersand Symbol

The Ampersand is a useful single character replacement for the 'and' word.

The ampersand is a powerful design figure. Its uses include:

1. Saving Space

2. Quick and easy
   to read

3. Changing fonts

Useful Tips

To create a perfect sign the letters need to be in proportion and correctly spaced.

It is important that it should make an immediate impression and be easily read. For instance, when it is to advertise an event or product, to give directions or a warning, certain words must stand out in order to grab the attention of the reader.

Here are three examples of how you can make a greater impact with a sign:

1. **Wide letters: Full square**

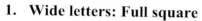

2. **Medium letter spacing: Approximately ¾ square**

3. **Slim letter spacing: Approximately ½ square**

Here are a few options in creating an impact and how to draw attention to certain words:

1. Use bright colours (especially on warning signs)
2. Outline or shade the important words.
3. Paint the main words larger (allow for plenty of space around larger words)
4. Always use legible fonts in proportion.
5. Chose your colours carefully to be seen from a distance.

I strongly recommend using quality brushes and materials in all your work

Sable
Writers
Brushes

Shown actual size

All of the exercises demonstrated and signs featured in this book were painted using the chisel edged sign writers brushes from the 2112 series shown here.

Sign writing brushes and sundries available from:

A S Handover

Unit 8, Leeds Place,
Tollington Park, London. N4 3RF
Tel: 020 7272 9624
Fax: 020 7263 8670
Email: adamvenus@handover.co.uk
www.handover.co.uk

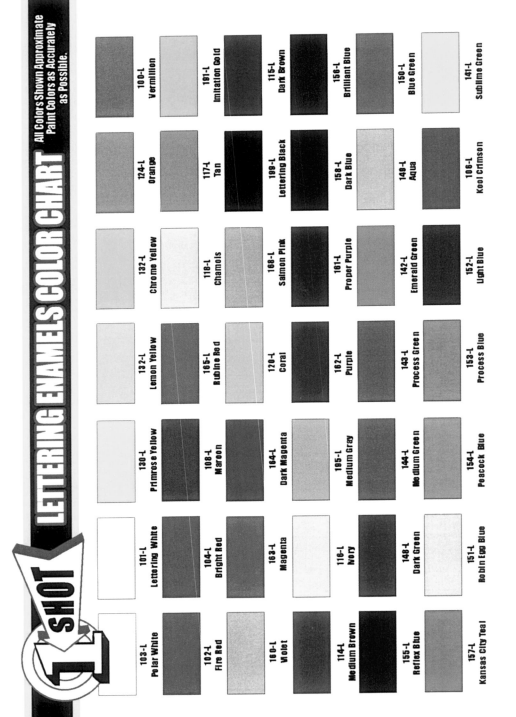

LETTERING ENAMELS COLOR CHART

All Colors Shown Approximate
Paint Colors as Accurately
as Possible.

1 SHOT

103-L Polar White	101-L Lettering White	130-L Primrose Yellow	132-L Lemon Yellow	132-L Chrome Yellow	124-L Orange	100-L Vermillion
102-L Fire Red	104-L Bright Red	108-L Maroon	165-L Rubine Red	118-L Chamois	117-L Tan	191-L Imitation Gold
160-L Violet	163-L Magenta	164-L Dark Magenta	120-L Coral	168-L Salmon Pink	199-L Lettering Black	115-L Dark Brown
114-L Medium Brown	116-L Ivory	105-L Medium Gray	102-L Purple	161-L Proper Purple	158-L Dark Blue	156-L Brilliant Blue
155-L Reflex Blue	148-L Dark Green	144-L Medium Green	143-L Process Green	142-L Emerald Green	149-L Aqua	150-L Blue Green
157-L Kansas City Teal	151-L Robin Egg Blue	154-L Peacock Blue	153-L Process Blue	152-L Light Blue	106-L Kool Crimson	141-L Sublime Green

For Information On
Workshops and Tuition
www.waynetanswell-signwriter.co.uk

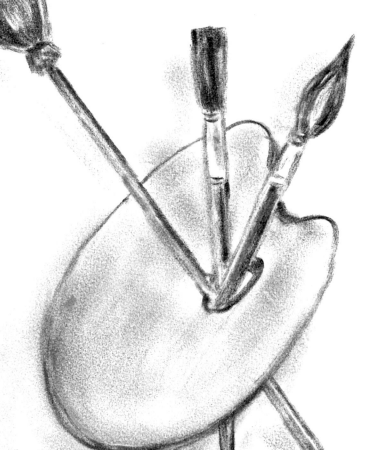

TANSWELL PUBLICATIONS
Learn How To Paint Signs (Introductory Guide)
Learn How To Paint Signs (Freestyle Guide)
Email w.tanswell@tiscali.co.uk

Signs of life

School sign painted by Gainsborough

Brush strokes identified as those of famous artist

Grammar Attack

A FORMER soldier is waging a one-man war on poor use of the English language after picking up a paintbrush to correct the grammar on his own street's signs.

Plenty of signs, little direction

Mix-up over painting on listed building

Sign reveals rich history of a village

Signs of revival